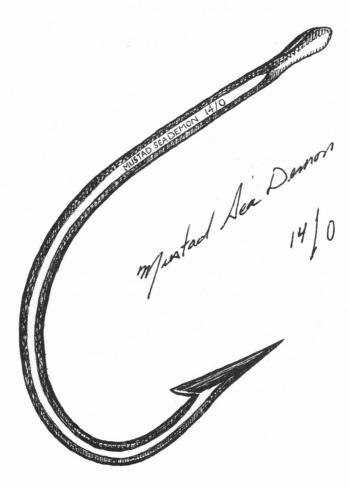

Mustad Sea Demon

14/0

On
Blue
Water

Art Lee

ON BLUE WATER

A Limited Edition
In Recognition of the Ernest Hemingway Centennial

The Beaverkill Publishing Company®

This book is published by The Beaverkill Publishing Company®

All Rights Reserved. Printed in the U.S.A.

For information contact:
The Beaverkill Publishing Company®
55 Riverside Drive
Roscoe, New York 12776

Library of Congress Catalog Card Number 99-94721
ISBN Number 0-9670639-0-6
Designed by Galen Mercer
Gimlets Are Good for Dreaming first appeared in different form in Sports Illustrated Magazine.
The Beaverkill Publishing Company® is a wholly-owned subsidiary of Beaverkill Productions, Inc®.

This is a Limited Edition of 1250 copies

Art Lee

ON BLUE WATER

This Edition is limited to
1250 copies
Signed by the Author

This book is for Santiago's Sail

CHAPTER II.

MARLIN OFF CUBA

BY

ERNEST HEMINGWAY

MARLIN and broadbill swordfish have been caught by commercial fishermen off the north Cuban coast for more than seventy years. Commercial fishing for marlin and broadbill was introduced by men from Manila in the Philippine Islands who brought the method of drifting with the current of the Gulf Stream in small but very seaworthy skiffs fishing a dead bait with from four to six heavy handlines at depths varying from seventy-five to one hundred and fifty fathoms. The Cuban fishermen — there are as many as seventy boats fishing marlin regularly within a distance of thirty miles each way along the coast from Havana — set out each morning during the season two or three hours before daylight and drift with the current of the Stream to eastward. When the northeast trade wind rises about ten o'clock in the summer mornings, they row their skiffs into the wind to keep their lines straight down from the limber sticks to which they are looped and which by their sudden dipping will show a fish taking the bait.

To Tommy Gifford who was catching them off of Cuba when we first began and who kept on catching them bigger and bigger from his friend and admirer

Ernest Hemingway

II

III

V

APOLOGIA

Captain Tommy Gifford had a book. It was one of 850 copies of *American Big Game Fishing*, edited by Eugene Connett and published by The Derrydale Press in 1935. In the book was a long piece by Ernest Hemingway called *Marlin Off Cuba*, subsequently shortened to run, I believe, in *Esquire* magazine as *Marlin Off Morro*. Tommy was very proud of this book, for in it was written the following inscription: "To Tommy Gifford—who was catching them off Cuba when we first began and who kept catching

on blue water

1

them bigger and bigger from his friend and admirer—Ernest Hemingway." While their admiration was mutual, Tommy more than deserved such a testimonial from the great writer and sportsman. For my money, if you were to ask who were the five greatest big game fishermen of all time, Tommy Gifford would rank 1st, 2nd and 3rd.

Years earlier, Tommy had taken me under his wing, not long after he and Johnny Harms, a Kansas farm boy who had found his way to the sea and stayed, were commissioned by Laurance Rockefeller to explore the waters around the Virgin Islands for billfish when Rockefeller was developing Caneel Bay on the Island of St. John. They found the fish alright and soon thereafter Johnny Harms built the Lagoon Marina at Red Hook on St. Thomas, and the rest, as they say, is history.

Shortly before he died, Tommy's wife, Esther, asked to see me. When we got together, she was carrying the book. Holding it out to me, she said only, "Here, Tommy would want you to have this." Without question this was the most moving moment of my angling career. Though a woman of few words and an independent spirit, Esther would never have made such a gesture without Tommy's approval, which in turn meant that I had earned Tommy's approval, which to this day means more to me than I can find words to say. I declined the book, however, suggesting instead that it be given to the IGFA library in Florida. It never was, I learned recently. And so I guess I should have taken it, for it wasn't until just last year, kindness of another thoroughly decent person, Judith Bowman, that those who love me—there are a few—were allowed to buy a copy (inscribed by no one but in pristine condition) for me for Christmas. It always sits where I can see it, and each time I see it, I think of Tommy Gifford.

I'm still not sure why Tommy should have taken such a liking to me. I'm not that likeable today and never was. But I do love to fish, always have, and I do care one helluva lot about how fish are caught. Cleanly and fairly and hopefully by people who share that view of what they are doing. On days when he had no charter, Tommy and I and whoever his mate happened to be at the time would put to sea anyway and begin the day by fishing for bull dolphin for the market to pay for the fuel. Dolphin love shade and so we would scatter a raft of pages of Charlotte Amalie newspapers over the surface of a likely spot, wait a beer or two, then try to hook up a fish on a feather and 100 pound monofilament line. As long as that dolphin stayed stuck, the rest of the school would hang around, and we'd catch fish after fish until the fish boxes were filled, the dolphin iced down. Then we'd go marlin fishing for the rest of the day. So I learned marlin fishing from the best without ever paying a dime and still from time to time go over the drill in detail in my mind just to be certain the fine points are never forgotten.

Most people who know me or my work think of me as a trout and salmon fisherman, unaware that I started what you might call "serious fishing" for want of a better word on blue water. I guess most people who see me and read me would say that my trade-mark—if you must—is a swordfish bill cap which I suppose some presume I affected to set myself apart from others who write about trout and salmon. Not so. I wear the hat and always will, or for at least as long as I can obtain them, because I started wearing it as part of the blue water uniform, and it's the best goddamned hat there is, or ever was, for fishing. Period. Tommy taught me that, and as usual he was right on the money. So, if this little book accomplishes nothing else, I dearly hope that clears up the hat business once and for all.

Indirectly, Tommy Gifford also taught me about giant bluefin tuna fishing, although we never fished together for that species. (We boated a few small ones together, but they don't count.) We didn't have to, really, so good was Tommy at explaining the fine points of anything that had to do with water, fish and fishing that if you attended, you could learn over the mahogany about as well as you could on deck or in the chair of almost anybody else's boat. Tommy Gifford boated the first 9 bluefins ever boated on rod

on blue water

and reel, cabled Hemingway who was living in Key West at that time, told him to get his ass over to Bimini and then the two of them boated the next 11 together. To boat either marlin or tuna in those days was really a feat because this was before Tommy had come up with the idea for the first anti-reverse reel, and so when a fish ran, the reel handle whirred backward at a commensurate speed. Hence the early big game reels being called "knuckle dusters," kind of an understated moniker, really, considering the amount of pain and permanent disfiguration they regularly caused.

Why you might ask was it Hemingway who Tommy cabled about licking the tuna? Certainly not because Hemingway was famous both as writer and he-man. To such a notion Tommy would have favored you with a one word response—"Bullshit."

on blue water

7

Tommy Gifford cabled Ernest Hemingway, as Tommy told me years later, because in his view Hemingway was the best man he could think of to do something new with involving blue water fishing. No less uncompromising than Gifford, Ernest Hemingway believed as Tommy did in the code of doing it as well as it could be done, learning as much as you could learn with each outing or not to do it at all. That our time might be summed up with the misapprehension that, "I think therefore I am," when it really ought to be, "I do therefore I am," is a fucking crime. Perceive the difference and you'll more than likely beat the tag. I hope I have, and if the balance between gut and reason I hope are put down here without pretense or equivocation and thus bring something to some-body—whether the said somebody, in Tommy's words, likes it Cape Breton cold or Bimini hot—who might otherwise have already missed it, is missing it now or may miss it in the future, then I will have done a job worthy of the paper and ink, the cardboard and cloth that go into making a book in this the 102nd anniversary of Tommy Gifford's first whiff of salt air and (just in case anybody on the planet has missed it) the Ernest Hemingway Centennial.

GIMLETS ARE GOOD
FOR DREAMING

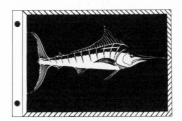

It's a mistake to ramble the docks and to see the defeated fish come in before you have fished for marlin yourself. Blue marlin that are strung up for the cameras don't look tough. They look black and dead, so very dead that it seems they might never have been alive. That they were beaten is obvious by their presence there, upside down with all those terse vital statistics painted in white on their sides—the victor's name, the date of the victory, the name of the marina for purposes of advertising, and if there is any room left over, the weight of the fish.

It makes more sense to unpack your bags, inventory your tackle if you have any and wait in a bar like Rumbottom's for the St. Thomas captains to come in. Listen carefully to what they have to say, say little or nothing yourself, and if you are sharp, you will get real insight into the sport from hearing that they love what they do, that they are challenged by it and that after all these years it still impresses them. They are like fighter pilots, or better yet, like navy chiefs. They are open and a little bit cocky or big and quiet and very, very strong. They respect strength and are inclined to ridicule weakness. They believe in God and they aren't crazy about having their pictures taken. After you have learned all this, if you have any sense, you should be just a little bit spooked.

Some drinks are better for staring into than others. Gimlets are very good. Martinis are no good at all. They look too shallow in the glass. Daiquiris are impossible. Trying to dream while staring into a daiquiri is to fool yourself. They are soupy and have little bits of vegetable matter floating about in them. Too cluttered for dreaming. Good judgment would tell you not to drink at all, of course, but if you are uneasy, as you no doubt will be, you will seldom show good sense about anything in any case, and so the best thing you can hope to do is to choose a drink with soul and promise like a gimlet to try to straighten out tomorrow in.

Tomorrow will be on you before you are ready for it. You will have to be jimmied from your bed or bunk, and after black tea and the tablet for seasickness you have secreted away just in case, you should walk to the docks, letting the tropics wish you good morning and good luck with smells you do not recognize and sounds you have never heard before. Your head will clear as you take it all in, and if you can say, "There's a first time for everything" and like what you hear, you'll be ready as ever for one of sport's greatest challenges.

The late charter boat captain Tommy Gifford used to tell of a gigantic blue marlin that showed on the grounds out of St. Thomas during the summer months when marlin fishing is best. Gifford was in his 70s then and swore to God he'd take on that fish one day and beat it. Tommy was built like a fire hydrant, cursed profusely and attacked billfishing in much the same way that Theodore Gordon took on trout. That is, he believed that the more you knew about the fish the greater chance you had of beating

on blue water
16

it. You owed a charter, your customer—a pretty fair euphemism as euphemisms go—no deference, which was the very best kind of flattery Tommy Gifford had to offer. To Tommy Gifford, charters were fishing partners and what you did when you fished together reflected on the two of you. If you blew it, he'd give you hell, but he'd go to hell to keep you from blowing it.

To Tommy Gifford, fishing marlin wasn't a game. If you didn't know how to take pain and like it, you could play golf. There was no place for you on board his boat. To make light of marlin or marlin fishing was to dishonor the fish and he'd see you shark bait before you got away with that. Not everybody liked it that way—neat. Not everybody cared that Tommy had done virtually nothing but fish since he was a little boy who caught striped bass at night by spinning squidding line around and around his body for want of a reel. And fewer still considered it a vacation day to be roughed up, hit upside the head with invectives (no matter how colorful) if you proved to be lazy or chicken, or worse, both. Tommy Gifford was the captain of his *Caribe Maid*, and if you thought you were out for a sail when you shoved off at 7 a.m. sharp, you soon found out that you had been shanghaied. Tommy believed there were "muscleheads" and there were "anglers," and by the lord who put you over the big fish, if you were the former when you signed on, you'd be the latter when you paid the tab.

Occasional big blue marlin are hooked—and boated—by novices, Tommy grudgingly acknowledged, but because he could list a hundred ways to lose a marlin, the odds remained very much against it if everybody aboard the boat played it square. But it would take special expertise and precision teamwork to boat the one giant fish that he lusted after and Tommy always promised to fish a full month with "a big Swede and a little Puerto Rican" he knew well and together they would prove once and for all that he didn't bullshit. The Puerto Rican, Tommy would tell you, had lived with marlin since he was a kid and could talk to the fish. The Swede, he'd say, had never seen a marlin in his life but had hooked many giant bluefin tuna from rowed dories on hostile seas and had more courage than any fisherman he had ever met. That promise may have been the only promise Tommy Gifford never kept. He died before he could get it done and was buried as he wished, at sea, between the Tobagos where he could forever look to the north toward the 100-fathom drop-off where it is certain his fish still swims.

From the marina at Redhook you take the

Middle Passage to the drop-off, a course between Thatch Cay, Grass Cay and Minage Cay. You leave the turquoise shallows for blue water looking down Drake's Passage west between the islands of St. John and Tortola where you cross the invisible line which separates American from British waters. You are making north across the grounds where sailfish abound in the fall and as you pass between the Tobagos you give a little salute and look up at the outriggers which seem to salute, too, for they are a marlin fishing innovation of the man who is buried here. You know that Tommy Gifford does not sleep. He is with you. A shoal of skimming flying fish that joins you on your way confirms that this is so.

It takes patience and great faith to troll for blue marlin. The rolling blue-waters of the marlin grounds are vast and your boat and your baits of cero mackerel or mullet or ballyhoo skimming the surface just ten yards astern seem very tiny in such vastness. You wonder how the big fish can find them, if they can see them, and why they would choose those particular baits when there are so many small fish in the sea. If you fish with faith, as you must, you sit in the chair squinting astern, your eyes roving from one bait to another not unlike a good turnpike driver checking his mirrors. "You're going to drill holes in the ocean," the skipper is apt to quip at you from the flying bridge. And you answer without looking away, "Maybe so, but I want to be ready." You probably should know that there is very little practical sense in what you are doing, since chances are that if a fish comes up, the captain on high or the mate with his practiced eyes will spot it long before you do. But then you think of the bible and wonder how well the skipper might know it. "Faith is the substance of things hoped for, the evidence of things not seen," it says. And for an instant you are tempted to quiz him on it but are intelligent enough in the end to think better of it. Instead, you wait and stare some more for things unseen.

There are almost as many ways for marlin to take baits as there are to lose the fish after they are hooked. The most common is also the most perverse and unnerving. The fish rises slowly behind the baits, feinting at each like a good boxer in the early rounds, then slashes at one, cuts at another, before finally taking the one in which it appeared to show the least interest during the seeming eternity it had spent in the boat's wake. More merciful but most shocking is the fish that boils up out of nowhere to angrily snatch a bait in one terrible turn—there and gone. It is awe-

on blue water
22

some. But it all happens so fast that you are in the chair and in the harness before you can really grasp what is happening, that it is to you it is happening to and not to some bronzed pretty boy wearing white terry-cloth slippers whom you might see in a promotional travelogue supposedly fishing for marlin without even breaking a sweat. Such is the stuff the officials of tropical islands seem to buy into these days as pitched by p.r. firms headquartered in New York, or of all places, Virginia. Most of all, though, you have no time to wish that the gigantic billfish trailing your baits would just go away and leave you alone.

The first ten minutes after you have driven home the hook belong to the fish. You belong to him, too. You are hanging on, pointing the rod at one of the most powerful and athletic forces that swims as it cuts the swells with the ease of a scythe in expert hands cutting through a field of brittle straw. Marlin have speed you can feel all the way down to your feet, and to believe for one second that you have any measure of control over one's first run would make you a fool, to try to do anything but to hang on and to hope the fish will settle soon would be to play the clown.

All good marlin fishermen must be just a little bit marlin themselves. There are some men who say they would prefer to watch others fight marlin than to fight them themselves, which is like you saying that you would prefer to watch someone else play Hamlet than play Hamlet yourself, or to listen to someone else conduct a symphony than to conduct the orchestra yourself, or to criticize rather than to paint, to read rather than to write. Fuck them all. For while boating a blue marlin may be more show for the observer than for the doer who actually sees very little while he is doing it, for pride of accomplishment in the absolute, there are few things in sport to equal being the one hooked up and in it from beginning to end.

After your fish has made who knows how many jumps that you sometimes can't be sure you saw at all and a little bit of the fight has gone out of the fish because it failed to knock you out early, the marlin should settle down some. It is then that you begin to try to wear each other down, and it can be a grim give and take. You will tell yourself a dozen times after a marlin has sounded that you will never be able to bring him back up and this can be profoundly depressing, perilously close to the border of despair. You find yourself praying just to see your fish again. But whether you do ever see it again or not, there will also come times, if you have any fisherman in you at all, when you will tell yourself that you are a man and that there is nothing a man cannot do if he decides to do it. Then in turn you find yourself wondering whether you really believe such a testimonial to the pride of man or not. Back and forth, up and down go your thoughts and actions. You ache. You want to quit and that scares you enough to give you the stuff to fight on, to ache some more. You pump and crank, gain and lose, until the overriding question ofttimes becomes what the hell you are doing there fighting to the death with this fish when it has always been so easy to enjoy fighting other much lesser fish to their deaths. That question you must purge from your mind in a hurry.

A good way is to recall how sickened Tommy Gifford appeared when he told of a professional football linebacker who had crumped under "a little fish," a two hundred pounder or so.   Gifford called him "a spoiled fucking brat who ended up actually begging somebody else to take the rod," and as you remember the curl of his lip as he told of it, you know for good and all that you wouldn't give up that rod now or ever for any sum and that you would kill the man who tried to take it from you.   And it is then that you know that you have found what it takes to win, whether in the end you win or not.

The big fish starts to come up, and you know that once it comes up it won't be able to go down again and that if the hook is well set, as you believe it is, you will hold him, you will be able to hold on, see it through. Suddenly the fish jumps once, twice, then rolls off the stern, light green and flaring as it turns its shoulder and side to you. The boat pitches in the rising swells of a little squall that cools you with the patter of rain on your forehead, across the bridge of your nose and down your shirt and your legs to your trembling ankles. The fish stares at you and you stare at the fish. You pump and reel. The marlin stands off.

"Put it to him" the skipper hollers from high overhead. "You're letting him rest. You gotta give 'im better'n that. Break his fuckin' back."

You believe, you truly do, that you're giving this fish everything you have and the captain's hollerings piss you off. You get mad. And so it has worked, for you do somehow find some more heave and some more pump and suddenly the mate has the wire and you are up and out of the chair and backing away to give the skipper and the mate room to bring the fish through the transom door. You feel a knot in your throat as the gaff socks him and yet you grin the biggest grin you have ever grinned even as your eyes are wet, and you almost feel sad, if only for an instant or two, that the battle is over and that you have won. There is always this worthy moment of sadness before the onset of ecstacy.

You hoist a salty blue-and-white flag with a marlin printed on it and listen to it crackle. You sit and stand and yak incessantly about your fish and how you beat the sharks that now surround the boat, drawn by the blood that was drawn by the gaff. You drink iced Flemish beer that burns your throat and although it may be no more than an average fish, 400 pounds or so, for some minutes you are the only man on earth who has ever fought and beaten so great a fish. In the marina you help with the hoist and watch the weigh-in and the vital statistics being painted on your marlin's side, and when the marlin is hung upside down, you pose for all the prerequisite pictures and answer silly tourist questions as best you can. And looking back on it later, you wonder if all of that is worth the price of being tough enough to defeat a marlin. You should promise yourself right then and there, while your marlin is still hanging and you can still hear the clucking shutters and the nasalness of your interrogators, never to kill another fish so wonderful again, unless perhaps with enough experience and expertise you are destined to be the one to take on Tommy Gifford's marlin among marlin and win. Then that night at Rumbottom's you should definitely drink daiquiris. They are the best drink you can drink to keep you out of yourself and off others when you have to do a lot of talking you don't want to do and getting very drunk seems to help.

on blue water

31

THOUGHTS FOR THE CHAIR WHILE WAITING OUT TUNA

If you were to swear that you are content today with the way it turned out, would they understand? Or might you not be wiser simply to cast your prospects of understanding adrift and ask them instead only to believe what you tell them because you have told it to them and because to believe you will not try them or cost them anything. To be believed is all you can reasonably ask for anyway, since even were each one of them to believe you, surely there would only be a few who would understand, fewer yet able to reckon whether your slant on it positions you among the luckiest or unluckiest, most blessed or cursed, of fishermen. For ultimately there are only two kinds of fishermen—those who fish for the fun of it and those who fish because they must, and unless they are like you, possessed of that ungovernable passion for the sport for its own sake, they cannot be expected to understand that it is how much you prize the challenge which counts and not whether you win or lose every time out.

Looking back, though, you have to admit it had never occurred to you that you wouldn't boat a tuna. There were plenty of fish around, and even before your first day out, boats flying tuna flags droned by your slip on the Annisquam River at regular intervals as they returned from Ipswich Bay to the north or Massachusetts Bay by way of Gloucester Harbor to the south. As they bubbled by, the swells from their wakes jogged *The Jealous Lady* just enough in her moorings to bring everyone aboard to the ports where you could plainly see fishermen and crews pitching drinks and slapping backs in pantomime, a ritual that varies little from successful vessel to successful vessel of the tuna fleet. And for long thereafter, there would be animated talk of tuna, the depths at which they were being marked, their great weights and matchless strength, the prices they were fetching from toothy Japanese buyers, all this mingling with the aromas of lobsters boiling, piss clams being steamed, grilling swordfish and sole being flipped in pans as you waited for a table at The Gull. All of it is reassuring, especially that ever-present hunch which some might mistake for misplaced confidence that, no matter how many disappointments you may have experienced in the past, tomorrow would belong to you. Faith and hope, two elements no less essential to any fisherman worthy of the name than a seaworthy boat and reliable tackle.

Nor can you allow yourself to be even a bit discouraged by the inevitable, if unsolicited, prophecies about the length of your odds as volunteered by some pessimistic Gloucestermen, usually unsuccessful fishermen themselves and almost always in their cups. You should learn quickly to ignore the chronic complainer, a type to be found anywhere there is water, who delight in buttonholing the visiting angler and trying to break his confidence with well-rehearsed, depressing reviews or fouled seas, declining stocks, apathetic politicians, and all manner of other drearinesses. Though much of it may be factual, these are concerns for other times in other places, and so your prospects for the days immediately in front of you are infinitely better served by pretending attention without really paying any, saying nothing, and looking around as discreetly as you can for sources of more encouraging discourse.

In any event, the mornings will buck you up, beginning with that vaporous pre-dawn darkness through which you plunge toward the docks fortified by the prospect of steaming black coffee. And then there is Joe Falconi, the skipper, waiting in the lighted cabin to assure you with his obvious calm born of experience of his determination to get you into fish. There is the tackle, the best stout rods that money can buy, gleaming reels, lines which have been checked and re-checked as though life itself might depend on them, wire leaders coiled and ready with heavy, lead sinkers painted flat black already affixed with dental floss, and great forged hooks honed to cut, bite and stay with absolute authority. There are the twin ice chests brimming with fresh herring and mackerel to be used for baits and strip baits, and tubs of bunker chumfish thawing in their own slime and blood from which you'll make the slick that is to draw the eternally hungry tuna to the baits against the traveling tides. And then of course there is *The Jealous Lady* herself, all 52 feet of perfectly proportioned elegance and practicality, the unchallenged queen of the Gloucester tuna fleet. Yes, you expect to boat a tuna, or perhaps two or three.

How well you read the odds of you getting a tuna once you are out on Massachusetts Bay, or wherever, and how decisively you and your skipper and his crew respond to that analysis as you turn to the hard pull ahead, has a lot to do with finally determining what kind of a team you will make. This fishing for bluefin tuna isn't like trolling for marlin aboard a solitary boat on a solitary slice of sea where your very solitude and the solitude of the sea seem somehow to attract you and your game to each other like companionless pilgrims in need of a gab. Instead there is a tuna fleet, many times hundreds of boats of every size and description with little or nothing in common beyond their floatability, which would appear to lurch without order in a seemingly coachless scrimmage over a small depression in the earth that happens to be filled with salt water and sometimes with fish. Although nobody really likes to say so, this fishing, with its endless jockeying for position in an attempt to give your boat an edge, the ongoing rosary of lies broadcast over radios, is really a high-stakes, if eccentric, competition as much between men on their boats and other men on their boats as between men on their boats and the giant bluefin tuna. Were the stakes not so high—maybe 20 grand a fish—perhaps it could be otherwise. But I've got to doubt it.

No, it is not ideal out there, and yes, you might change it some if you could. And yet there's something about it, something wildly beautiful and uniquely exciting, even aside from everpresent antic- ipation that at any second you may be compelled to test your skill, strength and endurance against the most powerful fish in the sea, an enormous fish, eight hundred, nine hundred, a thousand pounds or more built for speed, that restless, eternal wanderer ordained for the protection of the lesser fish of any given area to push on always against the currents of the oceans, Sisyphus climbing and re-climbing his hill. On the way out there is the summer sunrise, at first no more than a hint of pink where the black of the sky meets the black of the water, then a bold slash of orange stretching north and south from a rising, haloed ball that draws the sky and the surface of the sea into that huge flag of universe, world, place and you. And always there is the reassuring cadence of a swelling and retreating deck, the deep rumble of well-tuned engines, the smells of salt, that is, of landlessness, lingering exhaust mingled with that of coffee and tea, and of bait and of chum. A thousand private thoughts echo within your head, and there are glances exchanged among all aboard which speak volumes in the fundamental language of fishermen at sea. There are the colors, whiter-than-white whites, silvers more silver than silver, grays that buoy rather than depress, and more hues of blue, vivid and subtle, than any landsman could ever hope to see.

Best of all, though, you are reminded how much you love the fogs of tuna fishing, certainly not for practical reasons, but because it is with the coming of a fog when you are running on radar with the smaller boats chasing in your wake like frightened tots, that you are surest that this day will belong to *The Jealous Lady* and you because you are part of her. Other boats ghost in and out of view with each stirring and dying breath of breeze that moves the fog, and it seems to you a surety that there will be nothing to distract your tuna as it eats its way up through your trailing chum to one of your sweet baits. It is as though even all the hovering gulls are yours that morning, as though they too know you have arrived, that to play the percentages they should stick with you, for gulls, like rats, are too ugly not to be wise, and so will always stick to a winner.

You hear the silence carried on countless droplets that are this fog from far beyond where you ride at anchor. It is so deeply silent that each sound on board *The Jealous Lady* is amplified many times over normal, like so many breaking twigs in a forest at night. A fillet knife cuts chum, the crackle of your slicker with the coming of the odd gust of wind, rubber soles squeak on the deck, the touch of needle to paper behind the depthfinder's glass. Only the endlessly chattering radio contradicts the illusion of lacy isolation and even that, because the voices are ofttimes nameless and originate who cares where, serve to underscore an unmistakable and comforting sense of anonymity.

You are likely to mark your fish, one of a large school, long before it ever sees a bait. Four balloons, the flashy colors they were born with softened by the vapor, ride the surface attached to four lines that in turn are attached to four baited hooks. You may mark the school first at 130 feet, the fish swimming erratically into and out of the depthfiner's field of vision. In the chair—even as the balloons continue to bob gently and of course unaware of any potential changes in their future—you sit, short of breath suddenly, at once waiting, hoping for and dreading what seems to you at last to be the inevitable.

"90 feet," the mate sings out.

"C'mon," Your lips move but you cannot speak a word aloud. "Take it now, goddamnit or get the hell outa here and leave me the fuck alone."

"80 feet." the mate's voice brings you to your feet, one foot on each side of the fighting chair's footrest. A light breeze touches the balloons and they give a little wiggle. "75 feet," the mate shouts. "60 feet...55 feet...40. Willya look at that. 40 mother-fuckin' feet."

"Now, it's *gotta* be now," you plead under your breath, still standing astraddle of the footrest, but the balloons before you seem only to mock you with their apathy. "Now...Take it now or I'm going to bolt for the cabin."

For as long as you can remember—it seems forever as you fight back the panic that makes you want to get the hell away from that chair—there have been those four balloons bobbing out there on the skin of the ocean. You have counted them time and again, meticulously, in order from port to starboard then starboard to port. Four. Always four. One, two, three, four. Blue, red, yellow, green. Four, three, two, one. Green, yellow, red, blue. Four. Then how can it be that as you complete the count yet again that there are only three? One, two, three. Blue, yellow, green. Three, two, one. Green, yellow, blue. Dear Jeezus, where the fuck is red?

Then, as though as an extension of that question, the rod next to you in the chair plunges downward. And you will never forget the agonizing cry of line being torn off the reel and through the guides, your sudden and curious sense of relief as anticipation becomes reality, and a new anxiety as your new reality begins to settle in. There is an explosion of voices all around you, the cold metal of the rod butt in your hands, the line melting off the reel, the thunderous rumble from the bowels of the boat, the weight of the rod, the massive boil of *The Jealous Lady's* wake, the integration of absolution and exhilaration washing through you, the stirrings of your stubbornness coupled with an overwhelming sense of awe. In the small of your back you feel the harness being hitched up and it is welcome and you plant your feet even as the chair is turned by the mate to align you with the running fish.

But try as you will, you will never remember the precise onset of the nothingness. You refuse then and you will refuse always to come to terms with the line gone slack, how lifeless it is disappearing into the gray surface of the water under the fog, to confront the absolute loss involved in it, the absolute void of that instant, the ache of having failed yourself and Joe Falconi and his crew and *The Jealous Lady*. Of having been bested. It will only be with a little time and many words of consolation that you will begin to accept that you have just been bested by the best, that against the best you have given your best and the crew its best and *The Jealous Lady* her best and that you are no less a fisherman now than you were when there were four balloons afloat still astern. And that being one of those fisherman, you will understand that while your loss is terrible, it is not your first loss and it will not be your last loss, and that what it really is is but an interruption which has left you beaten now, yes, but defeated never, not for as long as you continue to breathe and you still have those hunches. And you continue to fish because you must.

Photography Acknowledgments

Frontis: (Top) Capt. Johnny Harms' Savannah Bay, courtesy of the Lagoon Marina.

(Bottom) Ready to do battle, steaming for Drake's Passage, courtesy of Kris Lee

Page I: (Top) Capt. Tommy Gifford courtesy of the Lagoon Marina

(Bottom) "The book," Tommy Gifford's copy of American Big Game Fishing as personalized to him by Ernest Hemingway, courtesy of Kris Lee

Page II: Ernest Hemingway and marlin, courtesy of The John F. Kennedy Library (Photo No. EH 2748P)

Page III: (Top) Broaching blue marlin, courtesy of Branniff International Airways

(Bottom) Giant Bluefin Tuna taking mackerel, courtesy of Aqua Marine Photography, Gilbert van Ryckevorsel

Page IV: The Gloucester tuna fleet, courtesy of Kris Lee

Page V: The author with 423 pound male blue marlin, courtesy of Kris Lee

Page 31 (Top) The author testing drag aboard The Jealous Lady, courtesy of Kris Lee

(Bottom) Giant Bluefin "on the drag" behind a commercial fishing boat off Gloucester, Massachusetts, courtesy of Kris Lee.

About the Author

Art Lee , the son of an avid saltwater angler, sold his first story at age 15, and with the exception of stints in the U.S. Marine Corps and as a newspaper journalist for The Hearst Corporation, has done little else but travel, fish and write ever since. During his lifetime he has caught virtually every fish that swims from bluegill to blue marlin. He and his wife of 30 years, renowned outdoors photographer Kris Lee, live in Roscoe, New York, the angling mecca of the Catskill Mountains.

OTHER BOOKS BY ART LEE

FISHING DRY FLIES FOR TROUT ON RIVERS
AND STREAMS

TYING AND FISHING THE RIFFLING HITCH

LURE OF TROUT FISHING

'KIN' AND OTHER STORIES (AVAILABLE SOON)

A Note On This Book

This book was set in Stone Serif , a solid, unaffected typeface the way, like a shotgun without a lot of extraneous engraving, the publishers felt Tommy Gifford and Ernest Hemingway would have liked it. The book was printed on Mohawk Tomahawk paper, easy on the eyes, and again, without affectation. The outside edge of the book was left untrimmed, a difficult process both for printer and binder today, as the single gesture to a largely bygone aesthetic. We would like to believe that Tommy and Papa would forgive us presuming to take this single liberty. The book was designed by Galen Mercer and Art Lee and composed by Susan King and Art Lee. It was printed by Prior King Press, Inc., Middletown, New York, and bound by The Spectrum Custom Bindery, Florida, New York. The cover engraving design , as well as the jacket illustrations and design, were executed by Galen Mercer.

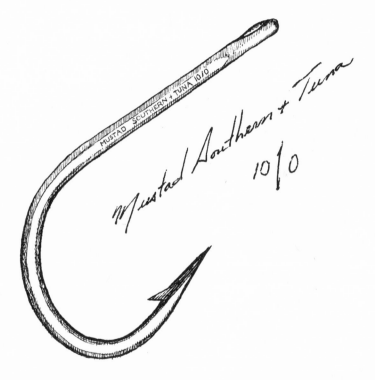

Mustad Southern + Tuna

10/0